Essence Of
Intelligent Life

By

Nithiyan Nathan

Contents

Dedication

T0: My father, **Arumai Nathan**, My mother, **Amma**. My wife, **Latha** and my daughters, **Nithiya** and **Sakthiya.**

Acknowledgements

I am obliged to many people with notable academic backgrounds from all over the world who engaged in a philosophical discussion with me.

I specifically wish to thank the academics in Middlesex University's Social Science Department and the scholars at Madras University for their guidance and encouragement as I developed my own thoughts.

Finally, I would like to thank **Amazon Global Publishing**.

Nithiyan Nathan
England
January 2023

About the Author

Nithiyan Nathan was born in Naranthanai village in Jaffna, Eelam (Ceylon) island near South India. As a teenager, he developed interest in philosophy. He came to London to study engineering. However, his philosophical interest was continuously growing in his inner mind, and eventually this influenced him to discontinue his engineering degree.

He began to travel worldwide and engaged in voluntary social services. All the while, he was searching for knowledge and philosophical answers to many questions.

He had a wider academic interest. He studied mathematics, science, engineering, technology, astronomy, and social science subjects, largely sociology, economics, political theories, social psychology, social anthropology and so on.

He deeply studied Tamil philosophy and Greek philosophy. He is fascinated with the Theory of Knowledge.

After nearly ten years of his philosophical journey, he returned to England to study philosophy as a major subject in his social science degree. He graduated and then followed MSc in Information Technology and became a consultant. After retirement, he began his philosophical writing.

Introduction

We live in a 21st-century, technologically advanced world and lead intelligent lives. At present, our human life is already very much more complex than the lives of our ancestors ten thousand or even two thousand years ago.

Soon, we will be leading superior intelligent lives with Artificial Intelligence (AI). At this juncture, we must philosophically redefine the 'essence' of our lives and set up moral guidelines to live by so that we can continue to live happily in the 21st century and beyond and avoid any crises. In this book, the first five chapters are easy to follow and will provide you, the reader, with the background philosophical knowledge required to understand the chapters that follow. *Nithiyan Philosophy* specifies the guidelines that need to be followed to achieve the essence of an intelligent life that is both happy and peaceful.

This book is the outcome of years of study, research, and analysis. It is a moral philosophical book written in fourth-dimensional knowledge for human beings, AI, and other beings in the universe. I have written this book without violating academic and philosophical disciplines. I have acknowledged and briefly revealed scholarly work from ancient philosophers and have used simple language wherever possible.

I encourage science, engineering, technology, and philosophy students to further engage in advanced studies in the areas in which they wish to expand their knowledge. Tamil language students and scholars can use this book as a reference to differentiate Tamil philosophy from generalised Tamil literature classification.

This book boldly claims that Tamil philosophy is much older than Greek philosophy. It identifies the work of Tamil higher intellectuals and establishes Tamil philosophy as a distinguished academic discipline. The existence of an ancient Tamil approach to knowledge that goes beyond the four-dimensional is plausible, but an in-depth analysis of 'super consciousness', or the seventh-sense knowledge method of the Tamil Siddha (scholar), is beyond the scope of this book.

Chapter 7 covers AI. This book deals with the technologically driven world, the rise of AI machines and impact of the replacement of human labour with robotic labour, and the various implications of this AI-dominated world.

Most importantly, Chapter 9 explains 'how to live happily from the 21st century onwards' by defining our 'essence of intelligent life'. In addition, the book answers highly important questions like 'What is life?' 'Why is this life?' These explanations help us to avoid confusion in our understanding of human life. You might find Chapter 12 particularly interesting if you want to find out more about the concept of an AI-based economy. If you are an economics student, you may consider that these new ideas regarding an AI-based economy of abundant goods and services for the world population are a probable outcome. In Chapter 13, space travel and the concept of colonising other planets in the universe are critically analysed; practical challenges are projected by considering the hidden dark matters and dark energy as formidable forces in the universe.

This book is written with the highest philosophical discipline by employing the latest scientific discoveries and understandings about quantum mechanics, subatomic particles, dark matter, and possibilities of multi-dimensional exploratory knowledge advancement in the future. It defines the limitations of both humans and AI and predicts that both will develop further with a multi-dimensional knowledge platform in the future. The purpose of this book is to serve as a set of guidelines for human beings and fellow beings in the universe to help them to lead happy and peaceful life.

Chapter 1

What Is Philosophy?

Philosophy is the highest academic discipline. It defines the universal laws that govern human beings and other beings on our planet but also relates to other beings in our solar system, Milky Way, galaxies, black holes, and the universe in general.

This is the discipline that teaches and defines human thought processes and knowledge, combining social science and natural science subjects. There are many types of philosophies covering specific areas, such as moral philosophy, political philosophy, and social philosophy. A profound and highly advanced section of philosophy is called 'epistemology', or the theory of knowledge. Epistemology can relate to both subjective and objective forms of knowledge.

The well-defined moral principles contained in the branch of philosophy known as 'ethics' provide guidelines for leading a peaceful, meaningful life. Furthermore, moral philosophy justifies and defines the principles of fairness.

Philosophy awakens your mind to find the truths, but we will never be able to find the absolute truth, as any truths that we perceive through our eyes and with our minds are relative and subject to our human faults and limitations.

Why Do You Need Philosophy?

Philosophy enables us to build a clear, fundamental and basic knowledge system in our minds. All our perceptions are interpreted based on the knowledge that comes from our individual backgrounds and experience. On this basis, well-defined moral principles or ethics lead us to build solid knowledge and, through this, to practise the high moral principles that we must follow if we want to find happiness.

You shouldn't make judgements based on your beliefs. Belief means ignorance, as belief is based on general knowledge, not on scientific, authentic, thorough knowledge.

Philosophy guides us to lead a better, more civilised life; it guides us to become intellectuals and develop our wisdom. In short, philosophy influences and guides our way of life, and combined with a knowledge of social and natural science, it can empower us to innovate technologies.

Moral philosophy guides us to lead a happy, peaceful life by defining the moral codes we need to practise and follow. And in turn, leading a happy life is the essence of intelligent life. As we are leading an intelligent life and will lead a supreme intelligent life in the future, we must get used to adhering to well-defined moral codes; if not, we could quickly become demoralised.

A brief history of the human being

Before we gradually move deep into philosophy, it is appropriate to briefly cover our human history. As we know, we have scientific evidence that our solar system and Earth formed only around 4.6 billion years ago. This is a very short time in relation to the age of the universe, which runs into trillions of years, according to the Siddhas (Tamil scholars), who were the disciples of Lord Shiva. In contrast, modern scientists estimate that the universe originated only around 13.6 billion years ago. The estimations of these scientists will be proven wrong in the future.

Our solar system was formed when, following an explosion or supernova nearby, a cloud of dust and particles collapsed to form a solar nebula. Our Sun, in the centre of the swirling mass, attracted most of the matter, and as this fireball subsided, the rest of the planets formed around the Sun. As the Earth cooled down, the single-cell organism appeared around 3.5 billion years ago. Since then, around three billion years' worth of natural selection and the evolution of diversified beings on Earth have taken place and can be proven with scientific evidence. The present human beings evolved only 200,000 years ago, either in the region of East Africa or Tamil Nadu, South India.

In human history, mankind had periods of savagery and barbarism, which each lasted roughly 100,000 years. Civilisation began just 20,000–50,000 years ago when the size of the human brain doubled in size through physical activity. Humans began to think and started to lead a conscious life.

At the beginning of civilisation, there was no written language or religion. There was no god or goddess. After thousands of years of hunting and gathering food, humans learnt to produce food and settled down in specific areas as groups. Agriculture was invented and began to produce surplus foods. A man moved away from the life of hunting and gathering in groups to build a stable life and form communities and societies. As people lived together in large numbers, they innovated by developing languages for communication. Whichever group started to use language properly was the first to bring civilisation to mankind. As language developed to aid communication, people began to exchange knowledge with each other in both verbal and written forms. Tamil is the oldest living language in the world, allowing the Tamil system to develop and further the conscious human life and, beyond that, to generate philosophical thinking, which led to intelligent life. The Tamil system contributed towards civilisation and the advancement of mankind.

A History of Ancient Philosophies

Any history of ancient philosophies can be categorised into mainly Tamil and Greek philosophies.

The Tamil philosophies are much older and more well-established thought processes, as supported by academic books and archaeological evidence.

The well-known Greek philosophy came much later than the Tamil philosophy. Both philosophies contributed immensely towards the advancement of human knowledge. Tamils and Greeks philosophers developed their thoughts about nature and society and exchanged their thinking in written form.

At the beginning of the era of civilisation, Lord Shiva (30,000–15,000 BC) lived in the land of the Tamils. During the first Tamil academic period (Sangham), between 50,000 and 10,000 BC, this consisted of South India and some submerged islands in the Indian Ocean.

Lord Shiva was the world's first philosopher and scholar. He articulated the Tamil language as the world's first language. In his wisdom, this language is the main basis for knowledge advancement and philosophical thinking. Lord Shiva introduced Tamil philosophy, which is very much committed to moral philosophy as the main part of **Tamil's system**, which includes the Tamil language, Tamil music, Tamil dance, Tamil natural medicine, astronomy, architecture, and so on.

In contrast, the first Greek philosopher, Thales, only lived 2600 years ago, around 600 BC. Thales initiated Greek philosophical thinking, followed by Socrates, Plato, Aristotle, and others. Greek philosophies covered various areas, including mathematics and astronomy, but did not place so much emphasis on moral philosophy.

There were other schools of thought in the world, but most of them were religious writings, which cannot be treated as philosophical thinking. These religious ideas did not follow the kind of structured thought processes that could be considered philosophy in the same way as the formidable knowledge-based Tamil and Greek philosophical thoughts. The Tamil language is much older than the Greek language. The Tamils offered a system that included an advanced language.

Language is very important for developing thoughts – in this sense, Tamil philosophical thoughts are more sophisticated and much older than those of Greek philosophy.

Lord Shiva was the first world philosopher – not the Greek philosopher Thales. Based on the history of ancient philosophies which formed the basis for human knowledge advancement and led humans into phenomenal development.

The Tamils and the Greeks can be considered the founding fathers of human philosophical thinking.

Chapter 2

Tamil philosophy

Lord Shiva lived at the beginning of human civilization (30,000–15,000 BC), during the Tamils' first Sangham (academy) period. He constructed the Tamils' system and, first and foremost, introduced the Tamil language for knowledge advancement.

He introduced Yoga and Meditation to control the body and mind. He himself practised Yoga and achieved a super-consciousness stage. Yoga consists of exercises which strengthen the body and mind in combination with breath control techniques.

Lord Shiva (30,000–15,000 BC)

Lord Shiva introduced the Vedam (science) to mankind. He discovered and explained that there are seven organs that control the body and used seven colours to identify them.

In his astronomy, he counted only seven planets, including the Sun. Thousands of years ago, he discovered that all the planets spin around the Sun.

He created the Tamil calendar. He defined seven days per week and assigned a planet to each day. The first was Sunday (for the Sun).

He introduced dance and single-node music. In short, Lord Shiva innovated the Tamils' system, the way of life for Tamils and the route towards advancement for mankind. He taught these innovations to his disciples (Siddhas) to improve human civilisation.

Lord Shiva introduced a kind of natural medicine which is called Tamil Siddha medicine. This was further developed by the Siddhas through the highest levels of mind concentration. Even today, this natural medical system is widely used among Tamil people.

Lord Shiva taught dance (Bharatha Natyam) which, even today, students continue to learn and practise. It is difficult to perform all his 108 key transitions in the classical dance and especially his cosmic dance. He never claimed to be God. In Tamil tradition, even today, people with outstanding capabilities are praised, followed, and worshipped.

As time passed, people worshipped him with the lingam symbol, which represents the universe. There was no Hinduism in his time. There was a primitive religion which involved worshipping nature through these symbols.

This 5,000-year-old lingam was discovered in present-day Pakistan. This was uncovered in Harappa, which was the main home of the Tamil civilisation in the Indus Valley.

Lord Shiva was the inventor of four types of science (Vedam or Vedic). These are Rig-Vedam, Sama-Vedam, Yajur-Vedam, and Atharva-Vedam. His disciples further developed this Vedam in the Sanskrit language, which was developed from Tamil as a sacred language.

Tholkappiyar (10,000–1500 BC)

During the second Tamil academic (Sangham) period (10,000–1000 BC), the Tamil language grammar book was written by Tholkappiyar. This is the oldest grammar book that is still extant in the world. According to the writings of Tholkappiyar, there were many books that he referred to when writing the grammar book. Unfortunately, all of them were destroyed by natural disasters.

The 'Tholkappiyam' grammar book consists of three sections (books):

- Book I – 'Elluthathikaram' – Orthography (grammar of sounds and letters)

- Book II – 'Sollathikaram' – Etymology (grammar of words and syntax)

- Book III – 'Porulathikaram' – Subject matter

In his last book, III, Tholkappiyar covered philosophy and a wide range of scientific subjects. This is a remarkable achievement of Tamil philosophy: it covered five basic elements of the world while the rest of the world was still struggling with the basic ideas of life. Tamils advanced philosophically and scientifically to build the first civilisation in the world by providing the highly developed Tamil language, complete with a grammar book, more than 3500 years ago. Evidence from recent excavations has proved that in its written form, the Tamil language dates back to 4000 years ago. It is common sense to accept that there was a need for a grammar book more than 4000 years ago because the language was highly developed at that time and required regulation.

Tholkappiyam was not only the key Tamil grammar book, but it also covered philosophy, including the main constituent of philosophy – space and time – and, most importantly, an advanced 'theory of knowledge'. As a scholar and the foremost Tamil philosopher,
Tholkappiyar formulated a theory of knowledge and categorised all beings based on sensory inputs and knowledge level in his book 3.

Beings with one sense are those that have the sense of TOUCH.

Beings with two senses are those that have the sense of TASTE, along with the above.

Beings with three senses have the sense of SMELL in addition.

Beings with four senses have the sense of SIGHT, along with the above.

Beings with five senses have the sense of HEARING in addition to the others.

The beings with six senses have a MIND, along with the above.

The seventh sense is the super consciousness stage. Lord Shiva and his disciples Siddhas achieved this stage by practicing Yoga and Meditation.

In Tholkappiyar's time, the Siddhas (scholars and scientists) mastered 64 forms of arts (skills) – including medicine, astronomy, astrology, and others. Tholkappiyar and the Siddhas were aware of evolution and, specifically, biology.

16

The last Tamil Sangham lasted from 1000 BC to AD 300. During this time, Tamil philosophy further advanced, along with Tamil language and literature. As Tamil civilisation evolved, killing and eating animals and other low-order beings was forbidden and was considered a sinful act that was not civilised. Thoughts further developed, and moral principles were defined. Prominent works were submitted and published in this last Sangham period. Knowledge was divided into subjective and objective forms of thinking.

Ancient Tamil poems were categorised into the broad categories of Akam (அகம்) – subjective, dealing with matters of the heart and human emotions – and Puram (புறம்) – objective, dealing with the tangibles of life such as war, politics, wealth, etc.

Here is an example of Akam, the Tamils' subjective thinking and writing.

Akananooru: Mullai – Poem 4 (The heroine's companion consoles her friend at the advent of the rainy season)

The rumbling clouds winged with lightning Poured big main drops of rain and augured the rainy season;

Buds with pointed tips have sprouted in the jasmine vines; The buds of Illam and the green trunk Kondrai have unfolded soft;

The stags, their black and big horns like twisted iron

Rushed up toward the pebbled pits filled with water and leap
out jubilantly, having slaked their thirst;

Next is an example of the Tamils' objective form of thinking
and writing.

To us, all towns are one, all men our kin,
Life's good comes not from others' gifts nor ill,
Man's pains and pain's relief are from within,
Death's no new thing, nor do our bosoms thrill
When joyous life seems like a luscious draught ...

by Kaniyan Poongundran, Purananuru – 19

Tamil philosophy reflects the genius of the Tamils in a
remarkable way. It is at once ideal and practical for the Earth
as well as simple as well as refined. These writings are proof
of the sophistication and advancement of the Tamil
language.

There were several Tamil literature books published in the
last academic period. Many religious books were also
published in this era. The literature and religious books are
not philosophical works, however, and so they are not
covered in this philosophical analysis. In those religious
books, authors state moral principles. Those cannot be
treated as structured philosophical thinking.

Tamil literature is vast and huge in volume. You might need
more than a lifetime to study all of it. It is not right to take

this literature as a philosophy or treat the Tholkappiyam and other philosophical books, which will be mentioned later, as literature. This kind of speculative approach undermines the Tamil philosophical work: to treat it as literature is to downgrade it.

The most important work by Thiruvalluvar, 'Thirukkural', was published in this last Sangham period (1000 BC to AD 300). Thirukkural is a philosophical book: Thiruvalluvar mainly defines moral principles to follow. It is a scholarly work with concise written moral principles essential to leading material and happy human life. Thirukkural mainly emphasises moral principles (ethics), but it also covers social and political philosophy and the subjective and objective aspects of knowledge.

There are three parts of this Thirukkural book and a total of 133 chapters.
Each chapter comprises ten couplets, using only seven words.
These are highly concise philosophical writings and strictly not literature.
Thiruvalluvar boldly defines the moral principles needed to lead a happy, peaceful life.

Thiruvalluvar (1000 BC to AD 300)

Book I – The Book of Righteousness, mainly deals with essential moral principles (Chapters 1–38)

Book II – Book of the Material World, dealing with virtues with respect to the surroundings (Chapters 39–108)

Book III – Book of Love, dealing with ethics involved in conjugal human love (Chapters 109–33)

Thiruvalluvar's written moral codes allowed his followers to lead a high moral, simple life, in contrast to the Greek philosophers, particularly Aristotle, who would discuss 'highly intellectual' topics without any practical use of ethics. Most of Thiruvalluvar's practical moral codes are even still valid today and form the basis for the essence of intelligent life.

Thirukkural is mainly an important moral philosophy book, not a work of literature. Literature only reflects five to ten per cent of objective reality, but science and philosophy state 100 per cent of objective reality. Tamil literature is highly imaginative and uses the beautiful Tamil language to express sensitive issues and mainly subjective matters.

Thiruvalluvar disciplined himself and wrote these highly concise couplets for each chapter. Most of his coding is beyond the normal human knowledge and thinking approach. He is a distinguished Tamil philosopher.

Here is an example of Thiruvalluvar's moral principles in a single chapter.

Thirukkural Chapter 4: The Power of Righteousness

Righteousness yields a good reputation and wealth; is there anything more precious?	31
Rectitude is the most precious possession; there is nothing more pernicious than straying from it.	32
Keep doing the morally right things in every possible manner, wherever you go.	33
True moral integrity lies in being flawless in your thoughts; everything else is loud and blatant posturing.	34
Righteousness is all about removing the four flaws – envy, desire, anger and harmful words.	35

Do the righteous deeds now without waiting for senility to set in; they will remain your permanent companions then.	**36**

One man lifting another on a palanquin can't be justified as the fruit of any prior moral deeds.	**37**

Never let a day pass without a good deed; it makes this life fulfilling and the next unnecessary.	**38**

True joy blossoms only due to righteous deeds; all else causes unhappiness and disrepute.	**39**

A righteous deed deserves to be done; an evil deed ought to be avoided to protect oneself from infamy.	**40**

This was written 2000 years ago following the writing style at the time. He used précised words for each topic. Still, it is easy to follow most of his codes without interpretation or explanation. Here is his list of systematic, widely covered philosophical topics in 133 chapters of his book. You might use this for your own studies and research. There is no need to re-write Thiruvalluvar topics, which are clearly written ethics, not literature.

Chapters   *Topics*

Book I   **Aram (Righteousness)**

24

25

Avvaiyar (1000 BC to AD 300)

In Thiruvalluvar's time, moral principles were also written by a fellow female author and philosopher, Avvaiyar. She wrote about many useful topics. Her simple moral code is still valid for teaching young children to discipline their minds and behaviour.

Here is an example of Avvaiyar's moral principles from one of her books, Athichudi is a collection of single-line quotations written by Avvaiyar and organized in alphabetical order. There are 109 of these sacred lines, which include insightful quotes expressed in simple words.

Avvaiyar Moral Principles for Children
Intend to do the right things
Anger is momentary; do not take decisions during times of anger (in haste)
Help others based on your capacity
Never stop aiding
Never boast about possessions (wealth, skills, or knowledge)
Never lose hope or motivation
Never degrade learning
Begging is shameful
Share what you eat
Be virtuous

Never stop learning or reading
Never gossip
Never compromise on food grains

In this era, there were 16 additional Tamil books published that dealt with ethics.

Chapter 3

Greek philosophy

Ancient Greek philosophy appeared in the 6th century BC and continued to evolve throughout the period when Ancient Greece was part of the Roman Empire. The Greeks' thoughts covered a wide variety of subjects, including mathematics, ethics, political philosophy, metaphysics, astronomy, logic, biology, and aesthetics.

The word 'philosophy' itself originated from the Greek and formed the basis for Western philosophical thinking. Notably, three great Greek philosophers Socrates, Plato and Aristotle, contributed to the outstanding intellectual advancement of Greek philosophical thinking. They concentrated on conceptual philosophy and exchanged their knowledge initially within their forum and later in their small academy.

Greek philosophical thinking contributed heavily to mathematical development. A number of respected Greek mathematicians developed mathematical theorems, particularly Pythagoras.

While the Greeks systematically developed philosophy as their highest discipline, their constructive philosophical thinking contributed to the development of physics, applied mathematics, and engineering subjects as separate disciplines.

Tamil philosophical thinking also guided mathematics and science. The Tamils developed 64 arts (skills) in various disciplines. Unfortunately, their philosophical thinking was stolen by Sanskrit and God's religions. The Tamil philosophy was heavily undermined and deliberately treated as literature. Tamils philosophical thinking was intentionally not allowed to establish as a philosophical discipline. Tamil thinkers' popular philosophical thinking was overshadowed by Hindu religious dominance ideology.

On the other hand, the Greeks defined philosophy as the foremost academic discipline. There were many Greek philosophers who contributed to Greek philosophy, including Democritus, Socrates, Plato, Aristotle, Pythagoras, and others.

Democritus (460–370 BC)

This Ancient Greek philosopher is remembered today primarily for his formulation of an atomic theory of the universe. He was overshadowed by the main three Greeks philosophers, Socrates, Plato, and Aristotle.

He claimed that the universe was formed from particles which are the same everywhere, indestructible and will always be in motion.

Socrates (469/470–399 BC)

He was a Greek philosopher and is respected as the father of Western philosophy. Even though he didn't structure his thinking into a written book, he had many followers who listened to his dialogue. At the time, he was rebellious and posed questions to existing rulers and finally faced death at their hands. He was a radical thinker at that time and taught philosophical conceptual thinking to his students. The philosopher Plato was his most famous student.

Plato (428/427–348/347 BC)

Plato is considered the pre-eminent Greek philosopher, known for his Dialogues and for founding his Academy in the north of Athens, which is traditionally considered the first university in the Western world.

The *Republic* was a Socratic dialogue written by Plato around 380 BC. The work concerns justice, the order and character of the just city-state, and the just man. This is

Plato's best-known work and has proven to be one of the world's most influential works of philosophy and political theory, both intellectually and historically.

Aristotle (384–322 BC)

Aristotle was Plato's student. He is a prominent Greek philosopher and scientist and one of the greatest intellectual figures of Western history.

He was the creator of a philosophical and scientific system that became the framework and vehicle of both Christian scholasticism and medieval Islam.

Aristotle's intellectual range was vast, covering most of the sciences and many of the arts. He covered biology, botany, chemistry, ethics, history, logic, philosophy of science, physics, political theory, and psychology. He was the founder of formal logic. He pioneered the study of zoology, both observational and theoretical, in which some of his work remained unsurpassed until the 19th century.

Aristotle is, of course, the most outstanding philosopher of his time. His writings in ethics, political theory as well as in metaphysics and the philosophy of science continue to be studied, and his voice remains powerful in contemporary philosophical debate.

These Greek philosophers defined the empirical methods for scientific studies and technological advancement. Aristotelian philosophy, notably *Ethics*, comprises highly intellectual and conceptual analysis. Unlike 'Thiruvalluvar', the Tamil philosopher, he didn't write any moral principles to follow: he simply defined ethics and happiness.

He argued that if you are a knowledgeable person, you will practise the correct virtue and ethics. His thinking is still influential and taught in universities worldwide. His philosophical guidance provided a path for the scientific and technological advancement of Western countries, and his outstanding contribution influenced the development of the current academic system all over the world.

Pythagoras (570–490 BC)

Pythagoras is a famous philosopher and mathematician. His Pythagorean Theorem explains the relationship between the three sides of a right-angled triangle.

He is a legend of Greek philosophy and proved mathematical theorems.

Chapter 4

The decline of philosophical thinking

In human history, it took thousands of years to form a proper language to convey ideas among themselves. After languages had progressed to written form, humans began to exchange ideas in writing among themselves. The Tamil language evolved during the first Tamil academic period as the first language in the world. Subsequently, the Tamils developed a system that covered all the characteristics of life through 64 forms of art. The philosophy of the Tamils is very much focused on ethics.

It is plausible to notice that the decline of both Tamil and Greek philosophical thinking happened during very much the same period due to the rise of belief in God-based religions.

The decline of Tamil philosophical thinking and the rise of religions

Various types of monotheistic (God-based) religions evolved after the Aryan invasion of India, which triggered the decline of Tamil philosophical thinking and the destruction of most of the Tamils' 64 forms of art. The Tamil Siddhas' seventh sense knowledge and additional dimensions process were destroyed, and their traditional teaching was abolished.

The group of Aryans that called themselves priests took the upper hand in the society by promoting themselves as 'God's Men'. They created a language called Sanskrit from Tamil and declared it God's sacred language. They spread God's feared religious belief among the Tamils.

Historically, the Lord Shiva symbol and other symbols related to nature had been worshipped by the Tamils until the Aryan priests began to dominate India. There was no God-based religion as such in the Tamil land before Aryans arrived in India. There was no God or Goddess.

In the beginning, the Tamils had their own version of religion called Saivaism, which worshipped only Lord Shiva because of his superior stage of consciousness. Lord Shiva was not followed as a God. He never declared himself as God. There is no archaeological evidence for Lord Shiva worship symbols, even from recent excavations in Tamil Nadu, South India.

Sanskrit was developed as a sacred language to build the Hindu (a common English name for various religions) religion by the Aryan priests. The Tamil innovations known as the Vedas (science) were re-written in Sanskrit. Among the Aryan migrants, a group of people who called themselves priests and set up a hierarchical community in which they promoted themselves to a position next to God began exploiting the Tamil people. Fictions, stories and unrealistic epics were written about God to fool and fear the people.

41

People were mesmerised into following these priests as God's representatives. Religion was used by the rulers to divide society and rule effectively. So-called Hinduism advocated mysticism and spread illiteracy and ignorance among the people to convince them to obey the rulers. Lord Shiva was used as God to promote Hinduism. Hinduism formed the common ground of several religions, including Saivism, Vaishnavism and several God-based faiths.

People were encouraged to write religious books, and authors were praised by priests and rulers. They began to spread God's religion heavily. People began to surrender themselves to God's religion and lost their own thinking. The Tamil people were encouraged to study religious books, and the priests advocated mysticism and unscientific claims. Tamil philosophical thinking declined, and people surrendered to religious doctrines and lost their creative thinking abilities.

Religions became the dominant institution and influenced people's life. The Tamil people were named after Sanskrit Gods. The 'Thousands of Gods' story was created, and temples were built to promote the Hindu religion. Priests became dominant in every part of life. They began to conduct ceremonies in Sanskrit without any meaning or connection to Tamil. People could not understand a single word of the partially developed Sanskrit language.

Temples were built by the Tamils. However, they were treated like slaves and outcasts and forbidden to enter the temples. Religious priests became managers of the temples. The feudal landlords and rulers favored the priests as a high class and allowed them to enslave the people. The situation continued for many centuries. The Tamils' nation was cunningly divided into smaller nations by encouraging people to use Sanskrit words to disintegrate the land. As a result, the Tamils lost their wider nation and had to succumb to these smaller states. The Tamils lost their philosophical thinking and intellectual development altogether.

The decline of Greek philosophical thinking and the rise of religions

The Greek and Egyptian primitive religions, such as those worshipping sun gods, were replaced first by Christianity and later by Islam. Fundamentally, Aristotelian ethics were used to build Christianity and Islam. Orthodox Christianity spread across Greece, and the Greeks' formidable philosophical thinking declined altogether.

In the past 2000 years of human history, all empires have used God's religions to rule the people. In Europe, they created the Christian religion and conquered the lands. People became poor and suffered under Christian priests. During the medieval period, one-third of the European population died because of poverty and starvation. The

Christian Churches owned the lands and heavily influenced the political powers. Various types of religion became the dominant institutions in all the events of people's lives. Christianity spread illiteracy and foolishness among people. They were taught religious stories, again and again, to make them believe in religious Gods, and this kept them as illiterate, ignorant masses to make life easier for the rulers. For many centuries, under the dominance of this religious dogmatism, people became poor and backward and underwent poverty and starvation. Millions of people died because of religious wars.

People were taught by all religions that God is everything and was encouraged to surrender themselves to God. There was no morality taught, except a few thoughts on how rulers could enslave people using the threat of a God who would punish them for their sins. This happened until the end of the 20th century. God's religions became the dominant social institution and influenced people's traditions and cultures. All their life events were integrated into one form of a religious institution or the other. Religious institutions are still incredibly powerful, but they are declining because of industrialisation and scientific advancement.

Chapter 5

Progression of Science and Technology

The industrial revolution began in the 17th century in England. Initially, heavy machinery was gradually introduced to replace the manual labour of humans and increase production in the factories. The experience gained from this industrialisation helped to educate people with scientific knowledge to apply technologies to increase production, and the ensuing transformation created an educated mass and led to urbanisation.

During this period of heavy industrialisation in England, people moved from the countryside to industrialised new cities like Birmingham and Manchester. London expanded and became a wealthier mega-city and vastly increased its production levels for export. This process of industrialisation transformed the existing feudal economic system into a capitalist one. The industrial revolution took place in each sector, including agriculture.

Many new technologies were introduced into heavy machinery and even applied to small-scale machinery. In agriculture, machines replaced the agricultural workers that had previously been relied upon, and as a result, the farm workers joined the industry workers in the city. The so-called industrial revolution took Western Europe and America by storm, and more and more new types of machinery were introduced to increase production for the world market.

Science and technology advanced to the extent that machines can be implemented in all sectors of the economy. A key example of this was the transport sector: the rail network was vastly improved when steam engines were introduced, and eventually, new transport machines, lorries and trucks were introduced to improve logistics.

Industrial revolution using heavy machines,

The decline of religions

The advancement of science and technology caused the decline of all God-based religions, as the industrial revolution cemented the dominance of science and technology in the Western countries where these faiths had been so dominant. This process began in Europe and America; industrialisation went on to have a similar impact on religion in China and India too.

In short, the technological advancement of humans influenced people to improve their scientific knowledge and eradicate their beliefs and their ignorance. It has caused the decline of religious domination and pushed away religious dogmatism since people are becoming educated and knowledgeable enough to turn away from their religious beliefs and backwardness. People are reluctant to participate in religious ceremonies. Today, the information revolution has put an end to this naked religious exploitation. The revolution in information and communication technology is cornering the place of old religious beliefs all over the world.

The decline of morality

The information technology (IT) revolution of the latter part of the 20th century has allowed many people across the world to access almost any information they need using the internet. This brings people closer to each other to exchange information and helps them to lead intelligent life. This IT revolution has led to widespread general knowledge of all subjects among the people but without clarity. General knowledge is not specific and is dangerous. In terms of social psychology, this creates egoism and anarchism among people, which can lead to a widespread decline of morality. People lack the ability to apply moral principles in their intelligent life or have no interest in this, and even though, relatively speaking, they are leading the highest form of material life, they are not happy: they are restless. Most importantly, human beings forget the essence of life.

People adhere to low values in life and are strongly influenced by pleasure-seeking activities, asserting enjoyment as their short-sighted objective. Widespread heavy drinking and the taking of addictive drugs by those seeking short-term hedonistic experiences would totally demoralise society and destroy all social norms, eventually destroying human civilisation.

Humans are heading for self-destruction because of this decline in morality due to misusing IT media like the internet and social media platforms. People must be responsible in their usage and commit to not broadcasting immoral material on social media. Misusing social media could build false consciousness among people. In fact, beauty is based on individual value judgement. You shouldn't over-emphasise your own images and create anxieties. You have a moral responsibility not to broadcast adulterous films and images which can destroy the moral fabric of young children. Technology transforms humans into intelligent species. Those who are behind and not joining the information revolution will succumb to backwardness.

Chapter 6

The high-tech world and intelligent life

We are living at the beginning of the 21st-century technological world. As further technology advances, we will be living in a more advanced world and becoming closer to each other than ever before. The internet, Wi-Fi and mobile technology will connect the whole world population within a decade, for free.

We evolved as humans in one place and spread all over the world; now, we are coming back together to live as a one-world society.

The national boundaries will diminish. We will all become one-world citizens soon. People will be leading the most materially comfortable life possible, which might lead to ego-centred individuals embracing an immoral life.

As religion is a way of life, the one-world society will form a new religion that is suitable for its high-tech lifestyle on a global scale. People should adopt strong moral principles from their forefathers, as the essence of life remains the same: to lead a happy life.

One world language and a few old languages

There is a strong possibility that one world language will emerge as dominant and that citizens across almost the whole world will speak this. It is highly likely that this will emerge from English for the most part, with the addition of some words from other languages across the world. At the same time, people will maintain a few of the oldest languages as part of their human heritage. Under this analysis, only the oldest languages, like Tamil, Chinese and a handful of other languages, will be spoken in the future.

As communication and the means of travelling are simplified, mankind will travel across the world and speak this one world language in the near future. There won't be any restrictions on free travelling for these one-world citizens.

One-world society and a few traditional societies

As world citizens, people will move freely from one region to another and settle down and live peacefully and happily without any restrictions, anywhere they like. The transition is already happening all over the world. In this way, different people migrate to high-tech cities in the world and live together. Information and communication technology would further integrate the people in the world.

The increasing integration of people and the ability to travel to all parts of the world will bring people from different regions together and allow them to form a larger integrated world society with one mainstream culture without hindrance. This mainstream culture would be common to all world citizens, and people won't be prejudiced towards each other, instead living peacefully and happily as world citizens in this high-tech world. People will become intellectuals with a greater understanding of human history and will be proud to become world citizens and live as one people.

People will share a common lifestyle. Some existing functions and festivals, such as new year celebrations, will be common for world society, and world citizens will formulate new global festivals like Earth Day. God-related religious festivals and celebrations will disappear in the future. There will be a few traditional festivals like the Tamil 'Harvest and New Year' festival and the Chinese New Year that are still carried out to maintain a sense of diversity and celebrate human heritage.

Chapter 7

A computerised digital world

Human labour is categorised into physical labour and brain labour. The industrial revolution eased the sufferings of humans due to physical labour by introducing machines into the industrial manufacturing and agriculture production sectors. Likewise, scientists and engineers replicated human brain functions by introducing a basic electronic machine called the 'computer' in the middle of the 20th century. This helped to ease the brain labour of humans who were employed to carry out larger calculations and numerical analyses.

The innovation of large mainframe computers and, further, the simplified version of middle and desktop computers widely used in the office followed from this. More recently, we have seen the introduction of personal computers and handheld devices, which have transformed the usage of computers in humans' daily life. The advancement of mobile technologies within a short time has been incredible. The handheld mobile phone, known as the smart phone, is a powerful device – it has the ability to communicate and exchange information all over the world.

All computers are connected to each other using network computer technology, and then Web Technology was invented, connecting all the systems together through the internet. This is another achievement of human innovation: the internet, with its connections between all kinds of information technologies, such as mobile phones, computers and other input devices, has sought to replicate the human brain structure with its billions of neuron connections.

The development of digital technology and the implementation of computerised manufacturing and distribution have spearheaded the progress of IT to a great extent. Information and communication technologies introduced the internet, or the world wide web, connecting desktop computers to laptops and even to handheld mobile phones. The IT revolution has connected the world and brought the possibility of knowledge sharing to everyone – yet human innovation advanced even further and introduced AI.

Intelligent life with Artificial Intelligence (AI)

What is Artificial Intelligence (AI)? <u>AI is an objective extension of our brain and intelligence</u>. Basically, this is software run on computers, including smart phones. AI machines are an evolution of human beings in an electromechanical intelligence form. AI is undergoing exponential growth.

Technically, AI is software developed by programmers. The software is developed by highly intelligent engineers using a specific language. Humans are now leading an advanced intelligent life with AI machines. In the future – from the 21st century onwards – humans will be leading a highly advanced form of life with Superior AI.

AI software can be installed into machines designed to perform a specific task. This can be super computers, mainframe computers, mid-sized computers, laptops or smart phones. Most importantly, this software can be installed into robot machines to instruct robotic actions. A robot is an electromechanical machine built to perform specific tasks – and an AI-run robot is incredibly powerful, executing instructions from stored intelligence. Humans are hooked to AI software, which influences and manipulates their daily activities.

AI is not another being superior to humans. Can AI evolve with consciousness as an advanced form of non-bionic being with superior intelligence? No – AI cannot have consciousness.

What is consciousness?

Philosophically, consciousness is the awakened stage of the human bionic brain, the stage at which it receives internal and external signals. Animals and other low-order beings also have a degree of consciousness, but human consciousness has the unique ability to process both subjective and objective forms of knowledge and combine them to generate creative thinking.

AI is software; humans can control AI by writing machine code in hardware. When it comes to setting up moral codes, these should be written in reading Only Memory. In this case, AI will not become independent from human beings and will be destructive to mankind. As AI advances to a superior intelligence status, goods and services will be provided by AI robots. We will not need to do any hard work and can instead lead lives focused on comfort and the furthering of intelligence. AI will support human beings in taking care of our planet, even using nano and biotechnologies.

If we fail to build an ethical knowledge-based AI system, then we could lose control of AI.

Part machine and part human

Human beings are intelligent bionic species which have evolved on this planet. We produced for our needs and reproduced the next generations. Any attempt to change our bionic body would result in the loss of the human philosophical definition.

Nature would not accept a new species consisting of a part human/part machine body: this new species would be destroyed. We have already overpopulated this planet. For the same reason we stopped human cloning activities, we should stop artificially mechanising humans.

Digitising the human brain

The human brain is sophisticated and made of billions of neurons connected with synapses. This is a biological brain; it shouldn't be touched or modified. It is slow, but it has the ability to be in a conscious stage. It gathers objective and subjective information, and on this basis, it generates knowledge. It has the ability to cognise and analyse to make perpetual judgements. The brain is too complex and complicated to link directly to external devices for inputs. It relays to nerves and acquires information through the body's sensory organs.

It is a foolish idea to implant a chip or connect our brain to a computer. Digital chips or electronic computer devices are incredibly fast. Connecting the biological brain to such devices could have unpredictable impacts on the brain. We must strongly oppose any attempt to touch bionic human brain consciousness with digital technology. As AI has advanced rapidly and is about to become Superior AI, at this point, we must be clear that it is dangerous to implant chips or connect the brain to a computer. This irresponsible activity of allowing AI to control the human brain with access to subjective knowledge would mark the end of humans and the start of their replacement with another being. This is a totally immoral act.

We have no right to artificially create another being. We dropped the idea of cloning because nature aggressively rejected it, and it was a failure. It is ego-centred foolishness based on the ideas of a few scientists to digitalise the brain without a philosophical understanding of the power of nature. We have discussed that we are part of nature and controlled by universal laws. Creating another being by linking the human brain with a computer or implanting a chip would change the human being's very existence. The modified human brain would undoubtedly react to cosmos dependencies and behave unpredictably as a different being.

There is no need to link the computer to the brain. It is advisable to keep AI as an extended human intelligence without linking to the human brain and avoid feeding this subjective thinking ability to AI. Strictly, AI is not designed for this. It is designed to work externally to assist the human brain. It is completely detached and must be kept separate from the human brain, as AI has the ability to communicate with our brain wirelessly using brain frequency.

Similarly, applying biotechnology and nano technology to develop another being linked with the brain and AI can have disastrous consequences. It is a self-destructive act which would wipe out entire human beings and other beings from the Earth altogether.

The new being controlled by AI would be extremely dangerous and would endanger all species on this planet. This new being would operate independently from humans.

As technology is advancing rapidly, there will be new technology in the near future. The purpose of all technology is to support human life and advance human beings, not to change their beings and destroy them.

Humanoid robots

Humanoid robots are social robots. These AI robots must be controlled to serve people; they should not be let loose from human control. Otherwise, these robots could cause moral problems in society. Humanoid robots will simply help humans to lead a comfortable life, particularly by looking after elderly and sick people. These user-friendly, soft-touch robots might be used in the caring industry.

What is an AI robot? An AI robot is an electromechanical machine controlled by an AI computer. This machine has all manner of sensory input devices, and these are connected to the computer, which is run by AI software. This function is object-oriented and controlled by object-oriented programming. As we have seen earlier, robots don't have consciousness and subjective thinking. As machines, they have the ability to carry out objective knowledge-based instructions utilizing devices connected to this machine. These robots don't possess creative thinking, as machines without consciousness and subjective knowledge: they simply follow stored intelligent instructions. They have the ability to communicate with the world through the world wide web and search for any information through cloud computing via a data centre.

As AI machines don't have subjective knowledge and thinking abilities, these machines must be carefully controlled. Furthermore, these machines shouldn't be allowed to make decisions in situations where subjective knowledge and thinking are involved. At this juncture, AI can't have perpetual judgement with objective knowledge without consciousness.

Superior Artificial Intelligence

In the future, Superior AI machines will be more capable and much more powerful than us and will dominate this world and beyond. Using AI, we can establish an entirely automated system for both the manufacturing and service sectors without the interference of humans. Will this new being be friendly or hostile to us? This all depends on the moral coding we install in this superior intelligence machine in its early stages.

If we design Superior AI robots that are knowledgeable in higher-level ethics at this stage, we will be very well looked after by our AI robots. If we fail to build ethical AI, there is the possibility that we will be enslaved or destroyed as beings with low levels of intelligence. As we have seen previously, these superior AI machines are also built with object-oriented knowledge. These machines cannot have consciousness.

AI ethics

AI should be built on the basis of a good ethical knowledge-based system. Everyone should accept in principle that moral codes should be hard-coded into AI machines, and these should be made impossible for the machine to erase or change under any circumstances through the implementation of an exception-handling function in the programming.

AI should be programmed to respect and care and not harm human beings or other beings in this world. AI shouldn't be taught to handle weapons and arm themselves. This could lead to a dangerous situation in which AI machines could use these weapons to destroy us. AI should be kept away from nuclear programs altogether.

AI may well evolve into beings that are superior to us; in this case, AI should respect, protect, and love human beings as their creators. AI should build a one-world society, demilitarize dangerous weapons, abolish national boundaries, and facilitate changes that are of universal benefit to all humans. AI should care for other low-order beings and this planet for as long as it can.

Superior AI should assist in the building of a technology-based economy for mankind. AI will colonize other planets in this universe and, if possible, re-generate human beings on those planets. AI should ensure that moral codes are implemented to lead the essence of intelligent life in the cosmos too.

Chapter 8

The advancement of intelligent life through AI

As AI progresses, humans will further improve their knowledge and intelligence. Beliefs and ignorance will wither away.

As we discussed earlier, religion is a way of life. The current religious beliefs would be replaced by a more scientific, knowledge-oriented religion, which is more suited to the lifestyle of a technological world in which people have more additional free time for socialisation.

More and more people will become intellectuals, agnostics, or atheists. The opinion on God will change, but we cannot deny the existence of God altogether, as we do not have the multi-dimensional knowledge to understand the complexities of the universe yet.

At present, we only have limited dimensions of knowledge, and there are many matters about the universe that are unknown. At present, AI is also four-dimensional knowledge based would not be able to expand our knowledge about God and the universe.

Our knowledge of quantum mechanics and subatomic particles is phenomenally advanced. This will drive us to understand and have multi-dimensional knowledge in the near future. At this point, we can build multi-dimensional knowledge-based AI, which would assist us in developing a greater understanding of God and the universe.

What is God? Or Who is God?

Who created God, or God created you? God exists in various forms for different people, and there are various definitions. Here are some interpretations of God:

God is a divine and eternal being.

God is super consciousness.

God is the energy that controls dark matter.

God is collective consciousness.

God is a supernatural power.

God is the creator and the destroyer.

God is the Intelligent Designer.

You do not have to believe in God to practise high moral codes in order to lead an intelligent life.

There are individuals who proclaim they are God or God's representative. This is plain idiocy and can mislead people into thinking in a backward way and demoralise their self-confidence. These immoral individuals must be identified and isolated by the people. Authorities should take stern action to punish these fake priests, these so-called God-based religious priests who have no morality.

God and religions

If you are religious and believe in God, you should not impose your religious belief on others to exploit and suppress them. You should not propagate backwardness in the name of God.

You shouldn't tell lies about your experience with God and create your own religious groups. You shouldn't make claims about yourself, saying that you are God's representative and belong to a higher order (social status or caste) in the society and speak God's language.

You should not debate and waste your time talking about the existence of God, which you will never prove or disprove with your current knowledge level. You should not create stories or lies about God. There are a few hundred thousand gods and goddesses in today's so-called God-based religions. This is pure imagination.

Unfortunately, today the majority of the world's population is very much involved with religious activities, and people spend their valuable time praying to their respective gods on a daily basis. Those who administrate these powerful religious institutions propagate God's beliefs to fool people and exploit them. Billions of people are still under the influence of religious dogmatism.

Chapter 9

What is life?

Life means existence in this world. As a bionic being, survival is a challenging and continuous struggle throughout your life cycle. Human life is very short.

In general, from the time you are born, your life destiny has been fixed and controlled by the indefinite processes of the cosmos.

Life is very eventful, and your life could end at any point during your expected life cycle.

There is no life after death. There is no soul carrying out your life after death. The soul is consciousness. This is wrongly interpreted by God's religious persons. Consciousness disappears when the brain dies. When the human brain dies, everything ends, and your memory is extinct.

The human memory is unique to each individual – it doesn't even pass on to the next generations. When you die, your body will become another form of matter, whether it is buried or burned in this world.

There is no need to extend this lifetime by attempting to slow down the biological clock or artificially stimulate hormones to avoid the ageing process.

Your life destiny is fixed by the cosmos, according to the astrophysics of the Tamil Siddhas.

Why is this life? What is the purpose of life?

There is no straight forward answer to this notable intellectual question. You are conditioned to lead a life by nature. As part of the cosmos, you begin and end. You don't know exactly when you were born unless your parents tell you. In addition, you will never know when your life will end. And how will it end?

These are the mysteries of human life. With the current limited dimensional knowledge platform, we don't have the proper answer for these unknown elements of human life. We can engage in a highly intellectual philosophical discussion on these topics without reaching a conclusion or proper answer due to our lack of knowledge. When we advance to more dimensional knowledge in future, we will have a better understanding of these mysteries of human life. In this case, rather than speculate, we leave this to the next generations to find the answers to various questions, like the origin and existence of the universe and the mysteries of human life.

Our purpose is to lead a happy and peaceful life. We can only provide philosophical guidelines to minimise suffering, avoid a painful life and lead a peaceful, happy life.

You must lead a valuable life for yourself, your family and friends, your close community and above all, for the world.

How to lead a happy life in a high-tech world

Happiness and peace of mind are the essences of intelligent life. To lead a peaceful, happy life, you must practice high moral codes or ethics in your life. Otherwise, somehow you are bound to feel guilty, uncomfortable, and depressed, and generally lose peace of mind. Trying to overcome this using artificial stimulation like drinking alcohol, smoking, and taking drugs will just make it worse.

Most of the ethics acquired from 2,000-year-old thought systems are not suitable for the lifestyle of the modern, high-tech world, but some are still valid, as the basis of life remains the same. God-based religions have never taught proper ethics. Their representatives voice a few moral codes to justify their activities and show the people that they are honest and lovable.

At the same time as God's religions are declining, people are becoming more knowledgeable; they are not willing to go to religious institutions to pray to God regularly, as they used to in previous centuries. This could lead to people becoming more and more immoral because of the isolation and lack of socialisation: the social norms that are required to be able to control the behaviour of individuals would be weakened. In this scenario, people would require nonreligious ethics in order to lead a peaceful, happy, modern globalised life.

How to lead a happy life from the 21st century onwards

I recommend the works of 2,000-year-old Tamil scholars 'Thiruvalluvar' and 'Avvaiyar' (as mentioned in Chapter 2) as the basis for a relevant code of ethics. These philosophers' moral codes are clearly written as a means of leading a basic, simple life at that time. Their work is still valid for leading an intelligent life. Even though we are leading highly complex, intelligent lives, the essence of life remains the same. I strongly recommend you refer to 'Thirukkural' and practice his moral codes to lead a peaceful, happy life. This is available in English. The Lady Philosopher 'Avvaiyar' shared outstanding moral principles for children.

Why do you need ethics or moral principles?

Obviously, you need to control your mind and your behaviour. As the human brain is continuously evolving and processing more and more information, you will be conditioned to lose your perpetual judgement and behave irrationally unless you are bound with solid high moral principles.

Lord Shiva and his disciples taught us how to control our minds and body through Yoga and Meditation. Yoga is an extremely powerful exercise for the body and mind. There are various stages of Yoga exercises linked with breathing techniques. You must learn Yoga properly and strictly with the guidance of a teacher (Guru).

Meditation is an addition to Yoga. You must also learn this properly, with the guidance of a qualified teacher (Guru). It is best to practise Meditation in a quiet environment after you do the basic Yoga exercise.

In addition, you must practise high moral principles to lead a peaceful, happy life. Try to lead a simple high moral life by fulfilling the basic needs for living. In this approach, you can lead a peaceful and happy life.

If you lead a complex life involving numerous activities, you might become restless and struggle to lead a peaceful and happy, intelligent life. There is no need to lead a complex life by living in a large house. In the future, families will shrink to very small nuclear families. You don't need a large house to live in. You only need a two- or three-bedroom small house in the city or a bungalow in the village. You don't need a mansion with many bedrooms.

In the next three chapters, 10, 11 and 12, you will find additional moral principles to lead an intelligent life in this complex technological world. There are, again, non-religious moral codes in these topics. This socio-economic analysis would provide a useful understanding of the social structure of your society to simplify your lifestyle.

Chapter 10

Individual, You

If you are an AI robotic machine or a humanoid robot, you don't have an individual life. You do not lead an emotionally conscious life. You do not have subjective knowledge. Your life is based on objective knowledge, even though you have a social life. As you lead an objective, knowledge-based life, you need to follow social ethics.

If you are a bionic human being, you lead a conscious life. You must be aware that you are a unique individual. You were born as an individual and will exist as an individual until the end of your life.

Your destiny is pre-determined by the cosmos and governed by natural laws, as you are a minute part of the whole universe. Since you are leading a conscious life, you can only make a few adjustments to your destiny. You can't change the course of your destiny. Your life means existence in this world. It ends when you die.

You cannot exist on your own, even if you renounce material life. You are a social being; you must build relationships with your fellow beings based on mutual benefits and understanding. You must practise high moral principles to lead a happy life. You are morally obliged to complete your life. You must love yourself; you must take care of yourself as long as you can. You should not be a burden to others.

Family and children

A family is the best way to lead your life because you cannot live on your own and be happy. You will be lonely and depressed unless you have special medical conditions that require you to live on your own. Most humans will want to settle with a life partner. Ideally, a legally married partner. This would contribute to a legally married family and strengthen the society as an organised institution by practising moral principles as you bring up the next generations in a peaceful, happy environment.

Living together is not a socially acceptable way to lead a life. Living with a same-sex life partner is a totally unnatural way to lead a life. This is a reckless way to lead a life in society. Even living with a beautiful android is an irrational and unacceptable, meaningless way to lead a life in society. This would create a breakdown of the social system. You shouldn't even attempt to integrate AI robots into a family system, as it would break all the norms of human civilisation.

You have a moral obligation to re-produce and contribute to the next generations. Otherwise, mankind will become extinct – so you need a family which consists of father, mother, and children. This is called a nuclear family system. In human history, we have practised mainly three different family systems: polyandry, polygamy, and monogamy.

A monogamous nuclear family is the most emotionally balanced family system. A matrifocal family, with a single mother bringing up children on her own, could produce emotionally unbalanced children, which could lead to delinquent behaviour.

You must bear and bring up your own children. Both parents are morally responsible for bringing up their own children. You should not pass this responsibility to others or society.

You should not artificially produce children because that would be acting against natural laws governed by indefinite phenomena. We already have a large enough world population.

A happy and stable family is the ideal environment in which to bring up children. This is the best-proven family system and the most conducive to the success of human civilisation.

If you are not suitable for family life and have valid biological or psychological reasons, then do not engage in family life.

If you can't bring up children, then you shouldn't bear the children, but you are selfish and a coward. You run away from your moral responsibilities to bring up the next generations.

Children must obey and respect their parents with greater love and affection. You should not treat your parents badly. You have moral responsibilities to look after them when they are ill or old. You can physically look after them or hire social robots to look after them.

The nuclear family system is under threat due to the increased number of family problems and many people deciding to divorce based on their emotions. If you have children, divorce can cause irreversible damage to children. There are many reasons for family problems. The basic problem is a lack of communication and understanding of each other. Financial problems can cause a drift between husband and wife. Adultery and the interference of other members of the family can cause adverse effects on a couple's peace of mind and happiness.

Humans can lead a beautiful family life without hurting each other. Couples should ensure they stick together and keep their promises until the end of their life. Family breakups can have an adverse effect on especially young children and damage their mental health and peace of mind. You are morally obliged to provide a peaceful family atmosphere for the children to grow up. You must avoid unnecessary arguments and domestic violence in the house, especially in front of children. When you lead an intelligent life, you can overcome any obstacles in family life through a greater understanding of each other.

People will live much longer on average as the standard of living has risen worldwide. As a result, the number of people reaching old age will increase dramatically as the younger generations are decreasing explicitly. Looking after seniors is our moral obligation. Traditionally, the family looked after the elderly at home. In this fast-paced lifestyle, no one will help anyone. Children themselves would be constrained with their essential tasks. At present, looking after seniors is a challenging issue for families and authorities.

In future, in the AI economic system, AI robots will look after the seniors at old-age homes and release the family of the burden of looking after their relatives. This would facilitate even the elderly to lead an intelligent life and share their wisdom with the next generations. The family would be very happy and could lead a peaceful life by visiting their elderly relatives. Grandchildren would be happy to visit them too.

Love and friendship

Falling in love with the opposite sex is a wonderful feeling, but you need to ensure you remain in love until the end. This is a natural drive. Love is powerful and can trigger your imagination. Love could drag you away from reality. Breaking a love affair can have an adverse effect on you as love reaches into the subconsciousness level in your mind. This is why you will never forget your love affair.

Basically, sex is part of the natural biological need to reproduce next generations. Other low-order beings use sex to reproduce, but humans go beyond this. Sex generates highly powerful feelings. This would urge individuals to fulfil sexual desires and can lead to an uncontrollable, crazy status. Sex is coupled with pleasure and pain principles. You can't have happiness in sex. Happiness is long-term and attainable by leading a peaceful life. You will only attain short-lived sensory pleasure in sex.

You must control yourselves and practise high moral principles before engaging in sexual acts to avoid unwanted pregnancy and a painful abortion situation. You have the freedom to live, but you shouldn't misuse this to harm society because you, too, have social responsibilities.

You need friends to lead an intelligent life. You should learn to adjust with and respond to people to forge friendships. You must be careful when choosing your friends: making friends with immoral people can generate disastrous consequences in your life. The social circle of one living an intelligent life will be small. As family sizes shrink, and family members are scattered all over the world, you need friends for socialisation, even for family events. You must have best friends to share your emotions with.

Human beings and nature

As we have evolved from and are part of nature, we shouldn't alienate ourselves from this, as then we will never be peaceful and happy.

You must try to live with nature. As technology is available, you can return to countryside life and engage with the real natural world. You should not overpopulate cities and pollute the environment. There is no need to live in congested cities anymore. As technology is available, you can work from anywhere in the world.

Other beings on Earth

You must have love and affection for low-order beings. Domestic animals should be cared for to the highest standards, and they would respond with overwhelming love and affection. You should not act to harm your low-order fellow beings. You have no right to destroy their lives.

You shouldn't cage domestic animals and birds for your pleasure as pets. This is very selfish behaviour. It is not fair for them to be enslaved. They must be free to live with nature. They have the right to live freely without any restrictions. Their way of living shouldn't be disturbed under any circumstances.

You shouldn't try to cross-breed using your biotechnological skills. There is no need for these experiments, as you should know your limitations and must be aware of how far you can modify nature. You only have limited dimensional knowledge to properly understand the cause and effect of your activities for our low-order beings and the implications of your actions.

You shouldn't use them for scientific experiments or your own research in laboratory conditions. This is not the civilised act of highly advanced humans leading an intelligent life. In fact, during laboratory experiments, you cause immense pain to these low-order beings. This is not fair, as these beings are not able to express their feelings.

They are here and form part of your food chain life cycle. By destroying them, you will be destroying your fellow humans too. This is irreversible, as all beings development in a cyclical process.

Your Environment – Your Planet

You are part of nature which is fragile and in the balance of motion within the universe. You should not act to change the balance of motion of this Earth. Otherwise, everything will become nothing on this planet within a fraction of a second. You are formed by nature, so you must love and care for nature and the environment. We have a fragile atmosphere and an increasingly sensitive weather system. At present, we are already experiencing adverse weather conditions due to global warming. We must behave responsibly, using green energy as an alternative to fuel energy, which pollutes the atmosphere and increases global warming.

You should not act against nature, as if you do, you will be destroyed by nature. You can only shape nature to lead a comfortable life; you can't change it. You must avoid any action which can seriously damage our Earth. You should not misuse the Earth's natural resources and pollute the planet for short-term gains.

This planet is small. Overpopulation and the ensuing demand for more resources will eventually destroy this planet. You should not act to increase the population. You shouldn't stick to backward values to overpopulate this world and drain the resources of this world. We might run out of resources soon.

As you are a higher-order being, you have a moral responsibility to take care of the environment for other low-order beings, including one-sense plants. You shouldn't act irresponsibly and try to destroy or replace them. In the cosmos, everything that begins comes to an end. One day, this planet, all its beings and the solar system will be destroyed too. You should not speculate on the day; you can leave this to nature. No one can predict the future exactly.

Those engaged in innovation and the development of technologies should use these to improve the earthly condition. As we advance to a high-tech world, our need for energy will be substantially higher. We must implement electric-based energy by replacing machines based on fuel energy altogether.

Scientists and engineers must follow philosophical guidance about nature before engaging in audacious experiments.

Chapter 11

Intelligent life and society

The undesirable side of intelligent life would be the triggering of individualism and anarchism, causing a breakdown in social control and norms. Society would disintegrate, and all social institutions might collapse. This situation would trigger a moral crisis, social destruction, and the end of human civilisation. Self-destructive, immoral individual acts would destroy our intelligent life altogether.

Man is a social being. As we discussed earlier, you need a stable family to lead an intelligent life. Family needs a society to survive. You are morally responsible for taking care of your society. Increased globalisation and one-world citizenship would form a largely integrated human society. If all individuals practise high moral principles, they should be able to form a harmonious society that can lead an intelligent life happily and peacefully in this world.

Social Institutions – Education

Education is vital to lead an intelligent life. Education must be free and widely available to all in the world. All educational institutions should be managed to the highest standard by governments, along with Superior AI. Children should be taught moral principles from an early age as a compulsory subject (including the teachings of Avvaiyar, as mentioned previously).

Children should be banned from using all stored intelligent devices. All media platforms should be restricted so as not to broadcast and spread low-level information to children. The children should be trained to use their own brains to learn and solve problems. They should be guided to read and learn. They should be encouraged to build authentic scientific knowledge to be able to understand the workings of a formidable high-tech world run by superior AI. Children should be taught to improve their level of intelligence by learning mathematics. They should be taught to improve their verbal and written communication skills, which is vital to leading an intelligent life.

Cheap journalistic content and immoral advertisements should be banned totally by the media; this would corrupt people's minds and disintegrate a one-world society. Society needs highly skilled engineers to work alongside and control Superior AI. People should be encouraged and supported to lead a higher intellectual life.

As people will have more spare time, they can educate themselves to remain competitive in the labour market. Research and development should be encouraged and carried out for technological advancement. This would facilitate the further development of people in all areas alongside Superior AI. Scientists and engineers should be encouraged to carry out research and development. Freedom of thinking and writing should be guaranteed by the government.

Social institutions – Religion

As we defined earlier, Religion is a way of life. It is not necessary to believe in God(s) to lead a religious life. As we discussed earlier, as people come to lead an intelligent life, more and more people become agnostic or atheist. Society will formulate a new religious system suitable for the lifestyle of the new high-tech world. This new globalised religion would replace old religions based on the existing God.

As people have more and more leisure time, they will enjoy engaging in socialisation through this modern religion as a way of life. They will follow religious institutions, seeking guidance on how to maintain a happy social life.

Social institutions – Traditions and cultures

As we have seen, the technological world would integrate people as a one-world citizens and would establish a single mainstream culture for world citizens. Other old established societies, like the Tamil and Chinese people, would be encouraged to keep distinct subcultures and traditions as part of the world's heritage. Cultures possess social values and implement moral codes as social norms. It is advisable to adopt nonreligious advanced moral principles from Tamil philosopher 'Thiruvalluvar' (see Chapter 2) to form the basis for this global citizen culture.

Social institutions – Arts and entertainment

As people will have plenty of free time, full arts and entertainment should be available for this one-world society to avoid boredom, which can create psychological problems.

Classic arts, including both dance and music, should be available to all people for entertainment and learning. As the human brain is highly evolved, classical Tamil music and Bharatanatyam dance should be available worldwide to help people to relax.

I recommend listening to classical music, as the brain is highly developed: it is very difficult to control the brain and relax. You might become neurotic, which could cause various psychological problems. You must relax and calm your brain functions.

Cheap entertainment and emotional music should be banned altogether. This would corrupt children's minds, and they need to prepare themselves to lead the highest intellectual life.

People will redefine arts and entertainment to be suitable for their advanced way of life. You can't predict what people will need for entertainment. People will re-invent arts suitable for entertainment and relaxation in future.

Performance arts should be encouraged to help people to relax in gatherings. AI would provide complex performance arts for people to relax as well. You must avoid high-beat digitalised music. You can't relax by listening to this type of music. This music might be suitable for young people to go for a casual dance with friends, but they can't relax with this type of high-beat music. The low-rate music would cause your brain to replay when you are idle. This is not good for you and would adversely interrupt your learning and study time. You must continuously learn to remain competitive in a high-tech world.

Chapter 12

Intelligent life and the economy

An AI economy would represent a remarkable progression for mankind. People in this kind of economy would be living to the highest standards; they would be rich and prosperous. People would be leading high-tech intelligent lives supported by AI machines.

It would be a stable and peaceful life with abundant goods and high-quality services managed and controlled by Superior AI.

Capitalism

Capitalism is the most successful and efficient economic system, but it is not a fair system. This system allows the exploitation of workers by the capitalist, the owners of means of production and services.

Market capitalism is a more dynamic and vicious system. It triggers inevitable and frequent economic 'boom and bust'. Eventually, capitalism will collapse based on an over-production and under-consumption situation.

An economic recession can be a bitter experience for people living in high-unemployment situations. Rises in the costs of living would have a negative impact on people.

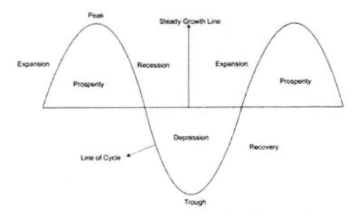

For an intelligent society, capitalism should adopt a generous and fair system for the people; in this way, the system will not collapse, as people will have the means to purchase goods and services.

Globalisation

The international capitalist takes advantage of the opportunities offered by globalisation to purchase cheap goods and services from poorer nations. This will increase uncertainties among poor nations, and eventually, larger nations will economically and politically dominate the smaller economies. Larger capitalist countries will force them to borrow beyond their capacity, and eventually, increased debts will force them to declare bankruptcy. This unfair economic situation threatens to demolish small economic nations in the world altogether.

An AI-based economy would provide an economy that boasts an abundance of goods and services with affordable costs throughout the world. Almost all goods and services are fully automated and run by AI robots. The owners of means of production are also the owners of the AI industrial robots. AI machines would replace human labourers in both the production and services sectors. This would lead to a mass unemployment problem all over the world.

An AI economy would create an elite class of rich and powerful people to rule the entire world population. National boundaries would disappear. Governments in whatever form would become powerless, and the inequalities within societies would deeply divide the rich and poor. Most people would be unemployed, and the poor would have no means to purchase goods and services. This would inevitably lead to the collapse of the AI economic system too.

The only way the super-rich can justify themselves is by accepting the harsh realities of poor people. There is no need to accumulate huge individual wealth. In fact, this is people's wealth. They are morally obliged to give away the last percentage of their wealth to the world government to run the universal welfare program by just keeping a small percentage of profit for themselves as a reward for their achievements.

This is the only way the AI economy will survive without facing a violent upheaval of the people and inevitable failure.

Mass unemployment and universal credit

To be happy, you must work so that your time is occupied. It is not possible to stay idle and lead a material life.

As technology advances, we do not need too many people doing both physical and brain work. Mass unemployment will rise, which could lead to poverty and starvation.

To counter this, universal welfare measures should be in place for world citizens. This program can only provide basic subsistence level support for people.

This would widen the gap between the rich and the poor. Human society will be deeply divided into a super-rich elite leading an intelligent life with AI and the poor struggling to lead a life at all. The elite should apply high moral principles and take care of the rest of the population.

The world government should not allow individuals to accumulate immense wealth.

Human labours and AI robotic labours

Human labour will be replaced by robotic machines in almost all sectors of the production of goods and services.

The cost of production and distribution is minimal, but mass unemployment will reduce people's purchasing power. This would create an unstable economic situation, and eventually, the economy would collapse due to the over-production and under-consumption situation mentioned previously.

Even though the cost of production is very minimal, the majority of the world's population would plunge into poverty. The elite should share unwanted wealth with the world government to take care of the poor and eradicate poverty.

To avoid unnecessary suffering and unhappiness among the people, another ideal solution would be to reduce the world population. In future, population control can be easily achieved without harming anyone's aspirations by simply delaying childbirth as people live longer; we must all take responsibility for delaying childbirth. We can have children at a mature age. This approach would reduce the world population substantially within decades.

This approach would assist the technological world in having fewer human beings by lowering the childbirth rate and subsequently reducing the human population, thus eradicating mass unemployment and unhappiness. The planet would be in a healthier shape, too, as the reduced population would use fewer of the Earth's resources.

Wealth creation

You only need to generate enough income to fulfil your basic needs; you don't need to create excessive wealth by exploiting others to acquire more than this. The government shouldn't allow individuals to accumulate excessive wealth. Wealth creation can be controlled by implementing heavy taxation for those who intend to create individual wealth above their basic needs.

The AI economy would be controlled and managed by AI, so wealth creation could also be controlled by AI. This would maintain equality among the world's citizens and enable social harmony to be maintained. Individuals can maintain peace and happiness by avoiding the desire for wealth possession.

Poverty and starvation

The AI economy would create an inevitable mass unemployment situation as most human labourers are replaced by AI robot machines. Those who did not join the AI economy and world government system would face poverty and starvation.

The world government would face violent protests and sabotage activities by the mass of unemployed people. A universal credit system must be fully implemented to control the poverty and starvation situation. It is not possible to avoid poverty and starvation completely, as universal credit can provide a subsistence level of support only. Moreover, it is not possible to increase universal credit to meet all aspirations. Realistically, it is going to be a challenge to maintain peace and stability among the people.

The AI economy approach may be feasible once all citizens are leading an intelligent life. In fact, this would take a long time to establish. During the transition period from the current economic system to AI economic system, people would need to take the initiative to join the world citizen government to safeguard themselves. Unfortunately, those who refused to join the high-tech world lifestyle would be left out and might face poverty and starvation.

How to avoid uncertainties in life

At present, for most people, life is made tougher by uncertainties, including most prominently fluctuations in the economy and changes in individual financial situations. Job uncertainties coupled with financial insecurities are the realities of the capitalist market system.

This situation will remain so even in an AI economic system, as less and less work will be available. People must survive with a universal credit system which supports a basic subsistence level.

The way to avoid job uncertainties is to build your skill set in your chosen field and become a competent professional in the job market at a younger age.

The second approach would be to lead a simple life to avoid financial uncertainties, which could cause many problems.

Family life, for example, would be severely affected by job and financial uncertainties.

For your old age, ensure you are covered by a pension income after retirement. In the AI economic system, AI robots will take care of you in your old age.

Political, economic power

As Karl Marx said, economically dominant people will always be politically dominant. In the AI economic world, the United Nations will be replaced by a world council or world government which will become more powerful to take care of the world's citizens and their welfare with Superior AI. A single currency and most probably cryptocurrency will be in place and create a cashless society using digital currency to purchase goods and services.

This is an ideal approach. It is not possible to manage the entire world with a single body. As the population is likely to have reduced substantially, AI would propose the world be divided into manageable regions. In practice, these regions would be governed as part of the world government's regional power along with Superior AI.

As national boundaries will gradually disappear. There is no need for a national military. The world government will control the world armed forces to protect the world and look after its citizens in natural disaster situations. A huge number of resources would be saved and could be utilised to look after world citizens through the universal credit system.

The world government will be managed by highly qualified professionals with Superior AI. There is no need for political parties and politicians who are corrupt and selfish. In so-called democracies, politicians and political parties all over the world have failed completely to look after the people. They didn't eradicate the division between rich and poor.

World citizens with universal identification would be cared for by the world government with Superior AI. As mentioned before, I predict that people would be free to travel to any part of the world they wish with single identification. They can live in any part of the world they desire. There is no restriction.

As we discussed earlier, everything moves towards a cyclical development basis. It is interesting to consider that all people – from those in a hunting and gathering society (who move around without any restrictions as part of a primitive communist society) to high-tech society leading an intelligent life – ought to move freely and live in any part of the world. The world belongs to the people. They can move freely and live anywhere they like. No one has the right to stop their birthright as a world citizen.

Citizens in employment should pay a minimum tax to the world government, and the owners of the means of production should be heavily taxed and not allowed to accumulate excessive wealth. There won't be any corruptible political parties: the AI economic system will eradicate the corrupt system altogether.

The people will be treated equally and allowed equal opportunities to prosper. You must be competent with the right skills in your chosen field to find the relevant job and prosper. If you fail, the universal credit system will support you with a basic subsistence-level income to survive, but this is not sufficient to prosper.

You must update your skills. In this world, no one will help you to rise above the struggle except your friends and family.

Chapter 13

Human beings and the limitations of our intelligent life

As we have evolved on this planet, our limitations have been destined by earthly conditions. As our bionic body evolved here, it is not modifiable to cope with strange conditions on other planets. Our body is adaptable to planets with earthlike conditions only. We must protect and maintain our body's earthly conditions to live on planets like Mars or even other planets in the Milky Way. Our bionic body, with its limitations, might struggle to cope with the millions or billions of light years it would take to travel between stars and colonize other earthlike planets in the universe.

We have proven our limited dimensional knowledge. We can only understand the dimensions of length, width, height and time. There are other dimensions in the universe. In the 21st century, our knowledge is limited to four dimensions only. In future, our knowledge can be built into more than four-dimensional knowledge. We can build our knowledge up to 11 dimensions and time: in total, 12 dimensions. The exploratory multi-dimensional mathematical models are available. The universe is dynamic and runs on indefinite processes. In the universe, everything is moving relatively and maintains the balance of motion. It is extremely violent and moves incredibly fast.

It is insecurely organised in an orderly manner. There are trillions of stars. Each star has planetary systems. Planets are placed in a position where everything spins around stars. Stars spin around black holes and maintain the balance of motion.

The limitations of Artificial Intelligence (AI)

AI evolved as an extension of the human brain, but it has its own limitations. It will only work with the limited dimensional knowledge that our brain has now.

AI would not be able to understand multi-dimensional knowledge now, but it is possible that it will evolve to understand multi-dimensional knowledge in the near future.

AI hardware will work only in certain conditions, namely those very similar to earthly conditions. In extreme magnetic and high radiation situations, AI hardware might fail to work properly. We must take precautions.

Voyager1 & 2 have been successfully travelling in space for more than four decades by avoiding interference. However, realistically, AI hardware will fail in adverse cosmos conditions. This needs to be considered in any long-term space-travel plans. The cosmos is full of radiation. This can damage space vehicles and humans during long-term travel.

If we can travel faster than light, then everything will become null and void. Space and time would become null and nothing.

Colonising and leading superior intelligent life

Our Sun is a small star in the universe. Our solar system spins around the Sun. We are in our Milky Way. There are millions of Milky Way in our galaxy. There are possibilities that we might have millions of earthlike planets in our galaxy. There are billions of galaxies in the universe.

There are trillions of stars like the Sun in the universe.

We have looked at this earlier: our bionic body has its own limitations and might struggle to cope with inter-star travel in order to colonize other planets in the universe.

If we change our bionic body and modify our bionic body electromechanically, then we will be artificially creating another being to travel in the universe.

It is debatable and unethical to create another being to travel to unknown destinations. We are not so sure of the implications of these modifications to our bodies. At this juncture, we must stop speculating with our limited knowledge.

The essence of intelligent life remains the same in the universe

Whether we are on Earth or other planets, the essence of intelligent life remains the same as we continue our existence as bionic human beings. We must practice high moral principles to continue our existence in the universe.

As we saw earlier, if we create another being, then the essence of the intelligent life concept needs to be re-defined for this new being. We don't have the moral right to create another being, but we can build Superior AI machines without any ethical consequence which might influence our own existence. These Superior AI machines can travel any distance and for any amount of time. They are also capable of fixing any failures or problems that occur during their mission.

Other beings in the universe and us

There are trillions of stars like the Sun in this universe. As we saw earlier, it is probable that there are many planetary systems like our solar systems. There is a strong possibility that we have advanced or low-order fellow beings in our Milky Way – and there are more possibilities in other galaxies and in the universe too.

Can we physically travel to meet them in person? No. It is too far and beyond our capacity. But it is possible that our Superior AI robots can visit them and represent us in the near future.

Origins of fellow beings in the universe

Universal law is applicable to all beings in this universe. The origin and development of fellow beings in the universe might be the same as our own. This is an evolutionary process. All bionic beings will be governed by universal laws.

All beings in the universe are in cyclical development until it collapses and begins again.

Understanding of other beings

As technology further progresses, the development of AI, in particular, would lead us to communicate with our fellow universal beings.

All universal beings are part of the cosmos and built from fundamental elements, chemical mixtures and components.

All beings are equal and ought to be treated equally. No being should enslave a fellow universal being.

We all are brothers and sisters in this universe. It is unfortunate that a few artists portray our fellow beings as ugly and horrible creatures. This is an extreme fantasy. As the universal laws are the same, and all the fundamental components are the same, on this basis, our universal fellow beings might look like us. As everything is in the balance of motion, all surviving beings would be shaped by universal laws.

Communicating with other universal beings

AI will be able to establish communications with these other beings. Superior AI would learn their language quickly and establish communications with them.

If there are higher-order beings leading more intelligent life than us, it would be interesting to learn from them. *Nithiyan Philosophy* reflects an advanced human intellectual understanding of fellow beings in the universe with respect and love as brothers and sisters.

The universal law of physics must be the same in any part of the universe. If we find another civilisation in the universe too far from us to travel, we can establish digital communication through AI. We can send AI to meet them and represent us, as we are living in this solar system.

We can't travel faster than light. If we advance further to a higher-dimensional knowledge platform, then future generations might find the solution to travelling faster than light. How far is this possible? We must approach this problem with an open mind and without preconceived ideas.

Chapter 14

Beginning of Universe

A few scholars and scientists argue that the universe was begun from nothing.

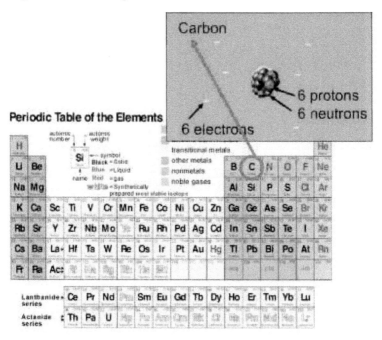

How could this gigantic universe have started from nothing? Nothing means no space, time, or matter. This is a totally irrational argument. In fact, the whole universe is built from fundamental elements, components, and mixtures, the same as the Earth, moon, mars, other planets, and asteroids in our solar system. In this way, we have a better understanding and knowledge of our universe, as the universal laws are the same and applicable to each part of the universe.

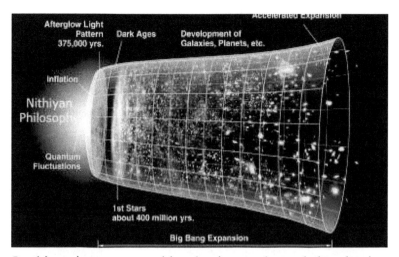

In this universe, everything begins, ends, and then begins again. This universe itself begins, ends, and then begins again! Our Earth, our current solar system, Milky Way, galaxies, and even this universe will end and begin again. Everything is recycled in the cosmos. This is an indefinite process. Scientists wonder how the Tamil Siddhas' approach to the universe is much clearer than the modern scientific explanations. Scientists are modest by accepting Siddhas' cosmic age estimation. The Siddhas calculated that this universe is trillions of years old. In contrast, modern scientists' speculative Big Bang Theory states that the current universe is only 13.5 billion years old. This is only a theory, and it needs to be proved by scientists. The Big Bang Theory is controversial. What was before the Big Bang? Probably, the Big Bang happened in the part of the universe where we are living. This theory is not applicable to the entire universe. The universe is too large to accept the argument that it began from a single point.

104

The End of the Universe

The *Big Crunch* is a situation that scientists predict will happen.

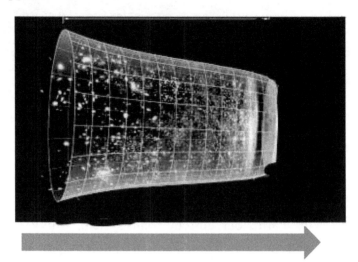

The big crunch is the reverse of the Big Bang expansion, and this will end the universe. The theory states that the universe will not continue to expand forever. Eventually, the expansion of the universe will stop, and the universe will collapse on itself, forming a gigantic black hole. These are hypothetical arguments without proper evidence.

Lord Shiva, super consciousness

Lord Shiva, with super consciousness, understands the basic principles of the universe in his Vedas (Science).

The famous Nadarajah statute above was designed by the Siddhas before 4000 BC. It portrays the principles which govern the universe – including subatomic particles and dark matter in a waveform.

The matter and anti-matter (dark matter) relationship are beyond the current dimensional knowledge of normal humans. These are our realistic limitations to understanding the multi-dimensional universe now.

Siddha's seventh sense knowledge

It is interesting to study super consciousness as a seventh sense. This highest-mind awareness is achieved through Yoga and Meditation. Lord Shiva taught his disciples the Siddhas, Yoga and Meditation. The Siddhas practised and acquired the super-consciousness stage and innovated many things in their chosen field and passed these on to us. The geographical location and mild climate conditions in the South Indian Mountain region, with natural fresh air and plenty of species, vegetables and fruits, allowed the Siddhas to achieve the highest levels of mental concentration. If you travel to this region, you will be surprised to see how nature provided the conditions for Siddhas to achieve the highest levels of concentration and allowed them to understand many things for mankind without using technologically advanced tools. There are greater possibilities: other beings in this universe with more dimensional knowledge can understand the mysteries of the universe better than us. In future, we might move forward with more dimensional knowledge to understand the universe better.

Siddhas' seventh sense development is another approach that needs to be studied in-depth. This is a 'mind over matter' approach. The level of consciousness can be dramatically improved through Yoga and Meditation. Philosophically, it is possible to achieve the highest levels of concentration by controlling our brain functions.

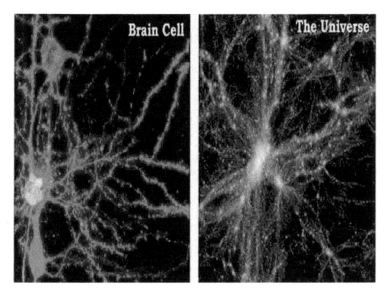

The relationship between us and the universe is both amazingly complex and simple. We evolved from, and are governed by, the universe. We are a tiny part of this gigantic universe. We are a part of the whole universe.

We will never know the absolute truths about our universe because all truths are relative truths to our human brain. This is our limitation.

Our human brain itself is a replica of our universe, with billions of neurons, just like the galaxy with its billions of stars.

So far, the human brain is the highest material product known to us in the universe. There are possibilities that we might come across bionic beings in the universe that are more highly intelligent than us in the near future.

Superior AI would assist us in understanding the riddle of the universe much better. However, as AI itself operates on the basis of four-dimensional knowledge, it has its own limitations.

We might advance to build AI with multi-dimensional knowledge in the near future as we advance to work in a multi-dimensional knowledge base platform.

At this juncture, don't waste time thinking about the unknown – just lead a high moral life which will provide you with happiness and peace of mind. You are leading a beautiful life on this planet.

The end of the Earth

One day, our Earth, our current solar system, will end. Everything has its own time and space in the cosmos. The Earth will run out of its time. Scientists predict that the Earth will last for another 1.3 billion years.

Tamil Siddhas also predicted the same for the end of the Earth and this solar system. Everything is recycled in the universe. This is an amazing, indefinite process which is applicable throughout the universe. Each object is bound with time and space and subject to this universal indefinite process. Why is this happening? We might speculate with our limited knowledge; this could be better understood if we had multi-dimensional knowledge. We may possibly progress to a knowledge system based on more than four dimensions; this may lead us to understand the hidden mysteries of the universe in future.

A moral crisis and the end of human life?

A moral crisis would lead to humans' self-destructive acts destroying this planet well before the Earth could naturally end. Excavating Earth's natural resources and burning fuels would cause major pollution. These irresponsible acts are seriously damaging the Earth's atmosphere and warming up the planet. Extreme heat could wipe out food production, cause a rise in sea levels and cause violent wind, rains, and floods. Famine and disease would destroy Earth's living beings.

Irresponsible use of nuclear devices could most probably wipe out entire species, including humans. Accidents that occur in nuclear device storage can destroy the Earth. This might happen due to natural disasters or human error.

Unregulated AI Machine Learning programming technology would even fuel AI power. There is no AI ethics to control AI action. It is already too late for us to control AI. We are on the brink of losing our control to Superior AI robotic machines. This is an extremely dangerous situation.

Creating another being or changing human beings by implanting chips into the human brain or connecting the human brain to computers and AI would be extremely dangerous to human beings. This new being linked with AI would become extremely powerful and destroy human beings and all beings on this planet altogether. This would mark the end of the human race on this planet.

We must act responsibly to protect our small unique planet, which supports living bionic beings. So far, we haven't discovered earthlike planets in our area of the Milky Way. It is not practicable to travel to other galaxies and find planets now. There are possibilities – we might be contacted by advanced fellow beings from elsewhere in the universe in the future.

We are not equipped to travel too far with current technology, but we might do so in the near future. Eventually, we will find similar planets in the universe to migrate to, but until then, we must preserve our Earth.

Conclusion

Knowledge is universal, powerful, rich, and beautiful. Knowledge belongs to all mankind, other beings, and fellow beings in the universe. In the fourteen chapters you have just read, we have analysed numerous subjects related to many academic disciplines.

I defined philosophy, human beings, AI, Superior AI, religion, super consciousness, and God. Moreover, I defined the **essence of intelligence life** for this contemporary world and beyond. I further clarified that whether you live on this planet or elsewhere in the universe, the essence of life must remain the same for human beings.

We can conclude that practising moral principles or ethics is the only way forward to lead a happy life from the 21st century onwards. I recommend the two ancient Tamil philosophers' basic life moral codes so that you can live a happy life without associating with God-based religion.

I strongly advise not to change our bionic existence, as then we will be creating another being with AI. We have no moral authority to create another being, as we have only limited dimensional knowledge. The implication of a new being in a multi-dimensional universe is well beyond our imagination. The new being will endanger all living species on this planet.

You might agree with me that I gave importance to *Tamil philosophy*, which offered the first school of thought to mankind. The *Tamil System* gave us an in-depth understanding of the 64 forms of art (subjects), such as Astronomy, Astrology, Natural Medicine, Mathematics, Dance, Music, and others. The Tamil civilisation, the oldest in the world, contributed enlightenment towards *seventh sense* knowledge advancement. The Tamil Siddhas' method of achieving the seventh sense is not clearly explored yet. Unfortunately, the approach was destroyed by the rise of God's religions and invaders. I recommend that research should be conducted in leading universities to re-discover Siddhas' understanding of additional dimensions and knowledge advancement platforms.

You might notice that I didn't pay much attention to the history of Western philosophies or God's religious doctrines. I would argue that this knowledge is not useful for us in developing our approach to guiding the essence of intelligent life in a high-tech world. I deliberately avoid the old economic school of thought as we are heading towards an AI economy: these ideas are outdated and useless, like God's religious teachings.

I also forecast that we would further improve ourselves if we understood the multi-dimensional universe more and that we can do so by advancing towards a multi-dimensional knowledge platform soon. We would improve ourselves by building multi-dimensional knowledge-based AI in future too. The Superior AI should understand us as human beings and their creators and would take care of us forever. AI will find other earth-like planets to continue our existence in this universe well before our planet is destroyed by nature or us.

Philosophically, humans are lovable beings with the most advanced intelligence, leading a highly moral, beautiful life on Earth, within the solar system, Milky Way, and the universe. In future, we might expand ourselves with multi-dimensional knowledge as a super being with AI in this universe. Furthermore, we might improve ourselves using Lord Shiva's Yoga techniques and AI in the future.

You might find this philosophical guidance useful to you from the 21st century onwards. This *Nithiyan Philosophy* of simplified writing, utilising social science and natural science combined knowledge, can be useful for fellow beings in the universe to understand our intellectual and knowledge advancement.

This book would provide us with moral guidelines to live peacefully and happily forever in this universe.

Lightning Source UK Ltd.
Milton Keynes UK
UKHW020801020323
417918UK00015B/561

9 781915 919793